PUFFIN BOOKS
LISTEN TO YOUR HEART

Born in Kasauli in 1934, Ruskin Bond grew up in Jamnagar, Dehradun, New Delhi and Shimla. His first novel, *The Room on the Roof*, which was written when he was seventeen, received the John Llewellyn Rhys Memorial Prize in 1957. Since then he has written over 500 short stories, essays and novellas and more than fifty books for children.

He received the Sahitya Akademi Award for English writing in India in 1992, the Padma Shri in 1999 and the Padma Bhushan in 2014. He lives in Landour, Mussoorie, with his extended family.

Ruskin Bond

Also in Puffin by Ruskin Bond

RUSKIN BOND

Listen to your Heart

THE LONDON ADVENTURE

Illustrations by Mihir Joglekar

PUFFIN BOOKS

An imprint of Penguin Random House

· PUFFIN BOOKS

USA | Canada | UK | Ireland | Australia
New Zealand | India | South Africa | China

Puffin Books is part of the Penguin Random House group of companies
whose addresses can be found at global.penguinrandomhouse.com

Published by Penguin Random House India Pvt. Ltd
4th Floor, Capital Tower 1, MG Road,
Gurugram 122 002, Haryana, India

First published in Puffin Books by Penguin Random House India 2022

Text copyright © Ruskin Bond 2022
Illustrations copyright © Mihir Joglekar 2022

ISBN 9780143453758

Typeset in Baskerville
Book design and layout by Samar Bansal
Printed at Thomson Press India Ltd, New Delhi

www.penguin.co.in

CONTENTS

'What I feel in my heart, I give to the world.'

—Franz Schubert

(1797–1828)

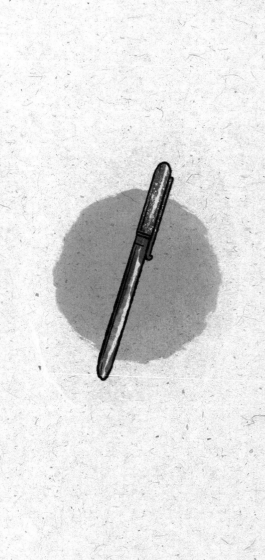

INTRODUCTION

This is the fifth (and final) memoir of my childhood, boyhood and early manhood—years that saw me grow into a young writer who, over the years, had his failures and successes like most of those who set out to make a living with their pen.

Today, it could be your laptop or thought-processing robot but for most of the last century it was the trusted ink pen. And with my trusted pen, I send my good wishes to aspiring young writers everywhere. May their adventure with language bring them joy and fulfilment.

Ruskin Bond

Landour, Mussoorie
23 February 2022

1

THE LONELY ISLAND

I was just seventeen when I arrived in Jersey, in the Channel Islands, in November 1951— ready to work for a living as best I could, but determined, above all, to write a book and become famous.

But before I could do anything about it, I went down with jaundice.

I had probably picked up the infection in the seedy, cheap Lamington Road hotel in Bombay, where I had spent three weary days waiting for the ship to sail. But two years earlier as well, at the school in Shimla, I had been hospitalised with jaundice. Years ago, my father had died of hepatitis, which was the same thing. So perhaps, there was a family tendency to be afflicted with liver problems. Whatever the cause, I had only been in my aunt's house in Jersey for a few days when I was overcome with fatigue and went yellow all over—as yellow as the haldi I'd brought for my aunt, and which had spilled out into my suitcase, ruining my two good shirts.

Uncle John (my Aunt Emily's husband) was a retired doctor from Lahore, and he put me to bed and treated me with barley water and light fluids. And after a week's rest, I was up and about, ready to explore the little port and resort town of St Helier, where my uncle and aunt had settled.

Jersey was an island about 46 square miles in size, the largest of the Channel Islands between

France and England. It was best known for its tomatoes, tourism, pretty bays and beaches, and of course, Jersey cows. The climate was milder than England's, but in winter, powerful gales often blew across the channel, and the fishing boats would take shelter from the heavy seas.

I was neither a tourist nor on holiday. If I was going to live with my aunt and uncle and their three sons (one working and two at school), I felt it was imperative that I find a job and contribute something to earn my keep.

I went about this in a very simple and innocent way. For several days in succession, I walked down the St Helier high street, knocking at the doors of the offices and inquiring if there was a vacancy in their firm. Most of them were legal firms and I had no legal knowledge or qualifications. The bigger shops and department stores looked more promising. I told their office manager that I could type; do a little shorthand; deal with correspondence; make bills and invoices; and add and subtract in pounds, shillings and pence. My efforts were

finally rewarded, and I was taken on as a junior clerk by Les Riches, a big department store with branches all over the island.

My uncle and aunt were astonished when I told them I had a job; they hadn't expected that I would go out on the streets looking for one. The pay was only £3 a week, but there was no income tax in Jersey. So I could give my aunt £1 a week towards my upkeep, and keep £2 for books, films, clothes and the trip to London that I had promised myself.

*

Les Riches made me work hard for that £3. Their office kept very long hours—8.30 a.m. to 6 p.m. It was dark when I left my aunt's shack on the hill, and it was dark when I returned to it in the evening.

There was the drudgery of keeping accounts and maintaining a ledger. The bench was cold and hard. The midday tea was horrible. The British love their tea, but they don't know how to make it.

Nevertheless, there was one saving grace. Twice a week, it would be my turn to carry the day's take to the main branch in a suburb called Georgetown. And after delivering the money, I was free to do what I liked. It seemed odd to be sending a boy on such an errand—carrying a bag full of money through the streets of a seaside town—but Jersey was relatively crime-free, and anyway, they probably thought I was expendable!

Georgetown had a small cinema that showed reruns of old British comedies, and after making my delivery, I would spend a delicious hour or two watching the antics of such comedians as

Will Hay (who wrote and played the role of an agitated schoolmaster), George Formby (who played the ukulele), Max Miller (who spent a lot of time betting on horse races), and Old Mother Riley (an actor called Arthur Lucan who dressed up as an old lady). These, and others, made me quite an expert on British film comedy of an earlier era.

But my evenings were lonely. I walked up and down the seafront, watching the tide come

in, the waves washing against the piers or going out, leaving the gulls to clear the beaches of the leftovers from visitors. But it was still winter, and there were few people around.

I was very homesick. How I missed India! How I missed Dehra—the old Station Canteen, the bazaar, the parade ground, my friends— Ranbir, his sister Raj, Bhim, Kishen, others— and our excursions, bicycle rides, the hot sun of summer, the monsoon downpours, the mango season, guavas, marigolds, birds in the banyan tree, tonga ponies trotting down shady lanes, the little railway station, watching the platform

recede from vision as the train took me away, sweet faces seeing me off . . . . Goodbye, goodbye! . . . Would I ever see them again?

The waves then came drifting in and I walked on.

While I was around so many people and the hustle bustle of the city behind me, I was still alone—a stranger in an unfamiliar land.

2

THREE JOBS IN A YEAR

It was kind of my uncle and aunt to keep me, and I got on quite well with my aunt. I would do my best to help her wash the dishes after meals, but I was so inept at this—often breaking her best crockery—that after some time, she refused my help and told me to stick to writing stories.

My uncle usually had his head stuck in the radio, keeping up with the latest political news. He was very conservative; never forgave the British Prime Minister Attlee for bringing an end to the British rule in India. His eldest

son, John, had strong views about everything under the sun, and would never admit to being wrong about anything, so I avoided getting into arguments with him. His younger brother, about my age, had no opinions at all; a morose, silent fellow. The youngest, Alan, was the friendliest. As he was too young to have grown up in India, he did not have the colonial mindset of the rest of the family.

After the family dinner, I would usually go up to my attic room and do some writing. Going through my diaries—the one I'd kept in school exercise books during my last year in India—I thought they might make for a memoir if I put them together after some editing and rewriting. I was good at writing 'set pieces'—the Holi festival, the break of the monsoon, crossing the Ganga— and if I developed some of the characters in my journal (friends, neighbours, shopkeepers, etc.), I might be able to blend all that material into a readable book—something between a novel, a journal, a memoir and a travelogue!

Till then I had only written a few short stories published in India. Now I wanted to spread my wings and write a book. I was not sure what kind of book, but there was no harm in starting one. My friends Somi, Ranbir and Kishen, and their families, leapt out at me from the pages of my diaries, demanding that I do them justice and bring them to life on a written page.

And so, my uncle and aunt did not see much of me except on Sundays. At Les Riches, even Saturdays were working days. Letters from my friends in Dehra were a great consolation to me. I longed to be with them again, and whenever I returned from work, I would see if there were any letters for me. An Indian postage stamp on an envelope always gave me a thrill, and I would hurry up to my room to find out what my friends were doing and to read their encouraging messages. 'You will be a big writer one day!' wrote Bhim. And, 'Come back when you are famous!' wrote Kishen.

I promised to do so. I couldn't return a failure. After three months with Les Riches, I found another job.

The London office of Thomas Cook, the travel agents, had sent one of their representatives over to Jersey to make bookings for the summer tourist rush. Her name was Mrs Manning. She had opened a one-room office in St Helier, and she needed an assistant. Some kind soul had recommended me for the job, and I was glad to take it. She paid slightly better than what I'd been getting at Les Riches, and the working hours were definitely more civilised.

Mrs Manning was in her early thirties, and as far as I knew, separated. She had a business-like manner and she was always well-turned-out. But she smoked heavily, in fact she was a chain-smoker, and the office was usually thick with cigarette smoke. I had never smoked in my life, and I had no desire to do so, but I had always been thrown into the company of heavy smokers—my mother, my stepfather, my schoolteacher Mr Jones with his cigars, and now my employer. There was no escape.

My job was to take phone calls from the London office, make hotel bookings as required and tend to any paperwork that Mrs Manning passed on to me. She was out a good deal, leaving me in charge of the Thomas Cook business. Being inexperienced, I made the occasional blunder—confusing twin beds with double beds, with the result that people who wanted to sleep together were being kept apart, and couples who preferred to sleep in separate beds were being bundled into the same bed.
Still, I was getting used
to the vagaries and
preferences of

human nature, when Mrs Manning decided to have a love affair.

She took up with a rather raffish gentleman who sold second-hand fire extinguishers. It was quite a scam. He would buy up old fire extinguishers, give them a coat of paint, emboss

them with a fictional trademark and sell them as new. It seemed a rather risky way of making a living, but he appeared to be doing quite well at it, and he was always bursting with confidence.

'Of course, it's a racket,' he told me on one of his visits to the office. 'But it's better than sitting in an office all day. Come along and help me with one of my demonstrations.' I declined the honour, but Mrs Manning may have accompanied him on some of his excursions. He boasted that he would cover every home on the island within a month.

Well, it was a small island, and he must have unloaded a lot of the out-of-date fire extinguishers on unsuspecting residents.

As Mrs Manning was seldom in the office, the London office got worried and sent someone over to check on our operations. He found me at my desk, working on my novel (there being nothing else to do between phone calls), while Mrs Manning's desk was taken up by a couple of freshly painted fire extinguishers.

'What are these for?' asked the man from Thomas Cook.

'They put out fires, sir.'

'I don't see any fires in this building.'

'They belong to one of our travellers,' I said truthfully.

That did not help and Mrs Manning was fired, the office was closed down and I was out of a job. Later, I heard Mrs Manning and her lover had moved on to the next island, Guernsey, where they were doing brisk business, selling naughty French postcards.

Before the debacle with Thomas Cook, I had, on an impulse, sat for the Jersey Civil Service Exam, open to anyone who had completed their schooling. There were only about two hundred candidates, and when the results were published in *Jersey Evening Post*, I found that I had stood fourth in the island, with a special recommendation for my knowledge of English literature (one of the four subjects).

My uncle was duly impressed. It meant a job in the civil service, at least a junior one. The salary was better than any I'd had so far, and my eighteenth birthday was celebrated with a

bottle of champagne, and a kofta curry and pilaf, specially prepared by my aunt; it made me even more homesick for India and my friends.

3

'I'M ON MY WAY!'

I was now a junior clerk in the public health department, but I had no intention of spending the rest of my life in Jersey, even if I rose to the dizzy heights of a senior clerk. Islands were not for me. All that sea, and a cold sea at that.

One day, I would return to India—this was a promise I'd made to myself—and in the meantime, my heart and mind were set upon London and the literary life. I wanted to emulate every writer from Dickens to Conan Doyle, but it would be a few months before I'd saved enough money to make the transition.

I was one of three clerks who took care of the weekly wage packets for the several hundred outdoor men who looked after the island's ancient but efficient sewage system. This underground world had inspired some literary masterpieces, including Gaston Leroux's *The Phantom of the Opera*, but it was not the sort of inspiration I was looking for, and my job was confined to the office. The sewers might have been a healthier choice, as my senior, Mr Bliault, was a chain-smoker, who puffed away all day, filling the small room with a cloud of tobacco fumes.

Still, Mr Bliault was an efficient accountant, much valued by the department, so everyone put up with his smoking and resultant coughing.

It was a friendly place and I got on perfectly with everyone. When the chief engineer, Mr Gothard, called me to his office on one or two occasions, he looked surprised when I addressed him as 'sir'.

'Did you go to a public school?' he asked me.

'Yes, sir,' I said, 'But in India.' I was to discover that in the UK, in Jersey and later in London, no one used the expression, 'sir' unless they were in a public school or in the army.

Let me share an interesting fact about the islanders. During the war, the Channel Islands had been occupied by Germany. Jersey had been taken over without any fuss, and when the war was nearing its end, the Germans left without any fuss. No armed conflict, no casualties. The islanders were a phlegmatic people.

They took everything in their stride, and got on with doing what they did best—breeding Jersey cows, fishing or growing tomatoes.

*

The first draft of my journal had been doing the rounds of a few London publishers, and coming back with polite comments and regrets. The post was usually delivered around lunchtime, and whenever there was a thud on the floor of the front door, my cousins would look up from their meal with a knowing grin, as if to say, 'Poor Ruskin, nobody wants his masterpiece.'

But along with the third or fourth flop of the returned manuscript came a letter from the editor at André Deutsch Ltd, a new publisher who was making a name and a reputation with some offbeat publications. The editor who wrote to me was called Diana Athill, and she wrote a very sympathetic letter, saying how much she liked the book and promising to reconsider it if I would consider turning it into a work of fiction, a full-fledged novel.

As a writer, I have always been ready to learn and to please those who encourage good writing, and I wrote back saying I would do as suggested.

There was no one with whom I could share this good news—my uncle and cousins would have considered it just another polite rejection. So I went out for one of my lonely walks along the seafront, and confided my hopes and dreams

in the waves as they came crashing against the sea wall. That island only came to life for me when it was blowing a gale. I loved leaning against the wind, feeling the rain stinging my face, listening to the roar of the angry sea as the tide came in.

As I walked alone down that rain-lashed pier, I knew I was going to be a writer—a good one—and that no one could stop me. The wind and the rain were allies; they were a part of me, and they would be a part of my work.

But it was to be a few months before I could launch out on my own, and during that time, I worked on the novel, pleased my employers and got on with my relatives as best as I could. My aunt never bothered me; in fact, she rather liked having me around. The youngest of my cousins was a friendly little chap; the other two rather resented me.

Whenever I had the opportunity, I went to the cinema, and one of the films released at the time was Jean Renoir's *The River*, based on the novel by Rumer Godden. This beautiful film made me so homesick that I went to see it several times, wallowing in the atmosphere of an India, a lot like the India I had known. The 'river', and its eternal flow became a part of my story too, especially the part where Kishen and Rusty cross the Ganga on the way back to their homes. And back in India, a young film-maker called Satyajit Ray saw *The River* and realised that a film could also be a poem, and went about making his own cinematic poetry.

With some help from my employers, I had acquired a baby portable typewriter, priced at £19, and I was going along quite merrily, working on the novel and keeping up my journal.

But then disaster struck.

*

Well, it wasn't really disaster. It had never been my intention to spend the rest of my life in

Jersey—London had been my destination—and what happened simply forced me into making my final decision.

Apart from working on my novel, I had also been keeping up my diary entries, and I had been foolish enough to put down some of my thoughts and feelings about my dear uncle, calling him 'Colonel Blimp', among other things.

'Colonel Blimp' had been a cartoon character from the time of World War I—a pompous, reactionary colonial type, the 'Burra Sahib' of the British Raj. Unfortunately, I'd left the diary on my

desk in the attic, and my uncle, prowling around, had opened it and seen what I had written. He summoned me to the drawing room and took me to task, accusing me of ingratitude and suggesting that I stay elsewhere if I was unhappy in his home.

Naturally, I felt humiliated and promised to leave as soon as I'd found accommodation elsewhere. I think he was expecting me to look for a room in St Helier, but instead, I gave a week's notice to my employers and booked a ticket on the Channel ferry to England. I'd saved up about £30, and I hoped that it would sustain me for a couple of weeks in London, until I found a job.

Well, I was beginning to discover that life isn't all about rewards and punishments, it's really about consequences.

One unplanned, unforeseen incident can change the course of one's destiny. If my uncle hadn't come across my diary entry, who knows, I might still be in Jersey, enjoying my pension from the public health department, while watching the fishing boats come in!

Instead, a week after the quarrel with my uncle, I was on the small steamer that plied across the channel, feeling quite sick (like everyone else on board), for there were strong winds and the sea was very choppy.

After being hurtled about by those rough seas for eight hours, we were set ashore at Weymouth, one of the south coast ports, and from here, I took the boat train to London.

4

LONDON DISCOVERED

It was March, and London was wrapped in fog.

And once again, I was looking for a job.

No, first I had to find somewhere to stay, somewhere to live.

A school friend from India, now working in a restaurant, put me up for two or three days in his cramped little bed-sitting room. From there, I moved to a student hostel—international, very noisy, with parties going on night and day, and very little sign of academic activities. I was a total misfit and I moved out in a hurry, having found a quiet and cheerful bed-sitting room on Haverstock Hill. The room even had its own bathroom, a rarity in London. And the rent, £2 per week, included decent breakfast prepared by my kind Jewish landlady.

I had lost no time in visiting the employment
bureau. The officer-in-charge asked me what
I could do, and I said I could type, write a letter,
do a little accounting and grow geraniums.
There was a job for a park attendant, he told me,
and it included outdoor work and cleaning up
the litter left by the visitors. It sounded tempting,

but when I looked out of the window and saw the cold rain pouring down, I thought an indoor job would be preferable. He looked through his index cards and said there was a vacancy for a junior clerk in a firm called Photax, but the salary was just £5, which was then the minimum weekly wage.

I decided I'd give it a try and went along to Charlotte Street, off Tottenham Court Road, where I found the showroom and office of Photax, a small firm making photographic accessories. The senior clerk seemed friendly enough, and when he found I was literate and reasonably intelligent, he put me in his accounts section. I was a ledger clerk again; dull, monotonous work, but not very stressful, and I knew I would be able to devote my evenings to my literary endeavours. This was to be my fourth job in two years; and once again, I looked upon it as another 'interval' or in fact my being on the way to becoming a full-time writer. But I would be with Photax for two years. Jobs weren't easy to find in the port of England. And writers weren't earning much either.

Meanwhile, the typescript of my novel (based on the journal I'd first submitted) was lying with the publishing firm of André Deutsch (whose editor, Diana Athill, had been so encouraging), and I was eager to see them as soon as I had settled into my room and my job.

I lost no time in contacting Diana and I was then invited to lunch with her and André. An author's lunch! This was a good sign. A publisher did not invite an author to lunch unless they planned to do business with them.

We lunched at a pleasant little restaurant near their Great Russell Street office. André was a small, affable man, who had escaped from Hitler's Germany just before the war. He had gone into publishing just three or four years ago, but he already had some successful writers on his list—Wolf Mankowitz with *A Kid for Two Farthings* (about to be filmed) and Mordecai Richler from Canada, and waiting in the wings were V.S. Naipaul and Jack Kerouac. Good writers were heading towards André Deutsch instead of the bigger companies.

Diana, by contrast, was a fairly tall woman, about my height, 5 feet 7 inches. She had a purposeful walk, auburn hair, clear spoken English (no funny regional accent), a slim figure and a persuasive manner. She was in her early thirties. Over the course of time, she was to become one of London's most respected editors and a writer of candid personal and literary memoirs. But at the time, she was relatively unknown, a junior partner with the firm; however, André relied on her when it came to discovering and publishing new authors.

The lunch went well, although I paid no attention to the food; I was anxious to hear what they had to say about my journal-turned-novel, the typescript of which had been with them for a couple of months. They complimented me on the book, told me it had been praised by the 'reader'. None other than the distinguished writer Walter Allen, who opined that I was a disciple of Sterne (I had yet to read Laurence Sterne), but that I should wait until I was older and more mature before rushing into publication. In spite of Allen's reservations, André was willing to take me on, provided I did some more work on the book—in other words, rewrite the whole thing! He offered me £25 for an option on the rights. I accepted. I was willing to work on that book again and again, so long as it could be published someday.

And I was richer by £25! Add to this my meagre salary, and I could afford going to the theatre occasionally and buying myself a new pair of shoes so that I could walk the streets of London in great comfort; for I was determined to discover the city on foot, as you could see practically nothing travelling on the underground railway.

There was no one to share my good news with, except my landlady, and she very kindly gave me a hot cup of cocoa to calm my nerves. But I needed something stronger. So I walked over to the best restaurant in Hampstead, ordered a martini and treated myself to an expensive dinner.

And later that week, I went to the theatre.

London was still the home of the theatre world; even the big Broadway shows came over to London sooner or later. And there were dozens of theatres and shows to choose from.

The first big musical that I saw was *Porgy and Bess*, the all-black folk opera composed by George Gershwin. This had some talented singers and great songs: *I'm on my way, Summertime, I got plenty of nothing, It ain't necessarily so, Bess, you is my woman now.*

Other musicals that came my way were *Guys and Dolls*, *Pal Joey*, *Paint your Wagon*, but these were anaemic compared to *Porgy*.

These were weekend treats. Every evening, after returning from work, I'd work on *The Room on the Roof* (for that was the title I'd settled on), writing, or rather rewriting a few pages before going out for a frugal supper at the nearest snack bar.

And in that process, my nineteenth birthday passed in solitary splendour. No one would have known about it, had not a couple of birthday cards arrived from my friends in distant Dehra, including one from Raj, the girl with whom I used to play badminton. I wondered if I would ever see them again. India seemed to be receding into a hazy distance.

My landlady saw the cards in my room, said nothing, but presented me with a simple sponge cake that she had baked herself. Dear London landlady, I don't even remember your name, but I remember your kindness!

*

Diana was kind to me too. She had me over for a meal occasionally (a wholesome English roast or shepherd's pie) and we would take walks in Regent's Park, and just across the road, exercising her pet Pekinese, Lichee. She shared her flat with a cousin, Barbara, a young woman of formidable talents who was to edit *The Economist* one day. Her fiancé was a writer called Anthony Smith, who travelled around the world in a balloon and wrote a book about it. She waited until he got back before she married him.

Although Diana was some fifteen years older than me, she seemed to like my company, and as we were both film buffs, we often accompanied

each other to the cinema. She took me to see a number of memorable French films—*La Ronde*, *Pépé le Moko*, *Les Vacances de Monsieur Hulot*, to name a few—and I took her to a revival of Marx Brothers' comedies at the old Everyman Cinema in Hampstead. I also took her to an Indian restaurant (there were half a dozen of them in London at the time) and persuaded her to eat a paan after the meal. I hadn't seen paan for a couple of years, and ordered it out of sheer nostalgia, but neither of us really enjoyed it and we did not repeat the experiment.

Then came the coronation, and all of London flocked to Westminster Abbey and lined the streets to watch the young Queen roll by in her gilded coach to be crowned Elizabeth II of England, or rather, Britain and the Commonwealth. Yes, the same Queen who reigns today, sixty-eight years on!

The winter fog was over, but of course, it was raining; and I spent the day in a local pub, watching the event on television. TV sets were just beginning to appear in pubs and clubs, the fare being limited to football matches, ice-skating extravaganzas, and public events such as the coronation.

Radio still ruled the airwaves.

And it was radio that gave me my first opening as a short story writer.

5

EALES' DISEASE

The stories I had submitted to magazines always came back. But when I took a chapter from my manuscript of *The Room on the Roof*— the episode in which Rusty plays Holi with his new-found friends—and turned it into a story by itself, it found its way to the BBC Third Programme (via Diana, I think), and was broadcast by that rather highbrow section.

It did not cause any waves—no fan mail! But it resulted in a producer from the BBC's home service asking me if I'd like to give a talk about growing up in India.

I wasn't going to miss such an opportunity, so I prepared a script that would last fifteen minutes, and took it over to the BBC studios, where I met my producer and the head of the talks department, Prudence Smith, and P.H. Newby, a well-known novelist and travel writer.

Prudence, a very kind and helpful person who had grown up in South Africa, took me in hand. It was to be a live talk, something I'd never done before, so we needed a bit of practice. My very strong Indian accent needed a little moderation—if I was not to sound like Peter Sellers imitating an Indian accent—and Prudence ended up giving me a lesson in elocution. All went well, and 'My Two Homes' went over the airwaves without a hitch.

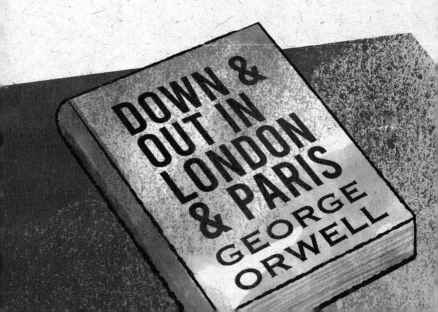

A month later, Prudence rang me up (on my landlady's telephone) and asked me if I'd like to give another talk. Naturally, I did so.

The BBC paid me at the rate of £1 a minute, so the two talks brought me £30. This, along with my 'minimum' wage (increased by ten shillings after six months) made life reasonably comfortable. I had been reading George Orwell's *Down and Out in Paris and London*, and I had to admit that London had been kinder to me than it had to Orwell. And as for Paris, it did not beckon. Victor Hugo had spent years of exile in the Channel Islands, and I'd had my share of them.

No, London wasn't unkind to me, but what I did miss about India was belonging to a 'family'—not necessarily my mother's and stepfather's home, but those several homes in Dehra where I had always been made welcome like another son of the house: Kishen's home, Somi's home, Ranbir's home. If you had a close friend, he was also your brother, and so, you were welcomed in the house as if you were another son of the house. Belonging to a family was something that I missed most of all.

And I missed the presence of children. Where were they—the Famous Five, William Brown, the Swallows and the Amazons, Billy Bunter et al.? Confined to schools or country homes, no doubt. Or did they exist only in books? In all my time in London (just over two years), I did not see any children! On one occasion, waiting in the hall

of a boarding house, I heard a baby crying, and presently, a pram was wheeled into the hallway, containing a bonny Punjabi baby!

On a Sunday afternoon, I stood before the statue of Peter Pan in Kensington Gardens, paying homage to J.M. Barrie, the creator of that eternal boy. At school in Shimla, I had buried myself in Barrie's plays—*Peter Pan, Dear Brutus, Mary Rose, A Kiss for Cinderella*—but here in England, I couldn't find anyone who read Barrie any more! It was as though I belonged to another era.

On Christmas every year, one of the theatres put on a production of *Peter Pan*, which would run for a fortnight during the festive season. That year, it was playing at the old Scala Theatre, just a short way down the road from the Photax office. Naturally, I went to see the play. Peter was played by the beautiful Margaret Lockwood, Britain's biggest movie star from the war years. Captain Hook was played by the Shakespearean actor, Donald Wolfit. I enjoyed the experience, as did most of the audience—all adults, wallowing in nostalgia. I must have been the only young person in the audience.

It was taboo to smoke in the theatre, but in cinemas, you could smoke freely. The screen was often observed through a thick haze of cigarette smoke. Smoking was Britain's national pastime, followed by the football pools. Most of my office colleagues read the *Daily Mirror*; the women loved a bit of scandal. I got on quite well with everyone, but I could tell that they thought I was rather odd for carrying a book around.

*

As the first summer hurried past, and the November fog closed in, I started having trouble with my eyesight. It was my right eye, actually. At first, I started seeing spots. Then, after a few days, the spots grew bigger. They became little grey clouds. Then after a week or two, they became one large floating cloud and I found that I had all but lost all vision in my right eye. As my left eye hadn't been affected, I could still read and write and attend to my office work. But it warned me and I finally went to my local general practitioner who directed me to an eye specialist. When the specialist examined my eye, he declared himself puzzled by its condition (apparently, there was some bleeding from the retina) and had me admitted to Hampstead General Hospital, where he could examine, test and treat me at leisure.

I was admitted to the general ward where there were about twenty other patients, most of them suffering from a variety of vague but troublesome ailments that were not responding to conventional treatment. The gentleman in the bed next to mine complained of a sensation in which he felt hundreds of ants crawling all over his body, even biting him from time to time. Another patient suffered from some sort of sleeping sickness, in which he slept all day but stayed awake and sang hymns all night; he was eventually transferred to a psychiatric ward. And there was a middle-aged Jamaican who complained of a variety of symptoms and was convinced that they were all due to someone's voodoo or black magic.

My eye surgeon was convinced that my trouble was due to some tropical infection picked up when I was in India. They did find amoebiasis in my system, but I told them that was very common in India. Even so, they gave me a course of emetine injection, which left me very weak. They also treated me with the newly discovered wonder drug called Cortizone, injecting it into my affected eye. This did not seem to make much difference. I was taken in a van to a distant laboratory, where photographs were taken of my retina, and these photos eventually appeared in the *British Medical Journal*, accompanied by a learned article by my doctor.

Eventually, after several days of tests and other procedures, some of them most uncomfortable, the specialist said, 'You have Eales' disease.'

'Eel's disease?' I responded. 'I've never eaten an eel. I've never even seen one.'

'No, Eales' disease,' he repeated, spelling it out for me. 'Named after a doctor called Henry Eales, who first discovered it.'

'Where did he discover it?' I asked.

This he could not tell me, but he did say that it was probably due to malnutrition and a deterioration in my general health. All those months of going without proper mid-day meals, living off Mars bars and beans on toast, had obviously taken their toll. For the remainder of my stay in the hospital (another fortnight), I was given some very wholesome and nutritious meals, which included a bottle of Guinness (a light dry stout) with my lunch.

All this at the expense of the National Health Service (a contribution having been taken out of my salary). I was the envy of the general ward. To add to my good fortune, I received a visit from the head clerk of Photax, who presented me with a month's salary. I was still on their payroll.

Other visitors included Diana who brought me flowers, and my landlady, who brought me one of her sponge cakes. I was beginning to enjoy my stay in Hampstead General. The nurses were good-humoured and friendly. The book trolley came around every afternoon, and I discovered the stories of William Saroyan, the crime novels of Josephine Tey, and wartime novels of Nigel Balchin and F.L. Green.[1]

---

[1] William Saroyan: *My Name Is Aram*
Josephine Tey: *The Daughter of Time*
Nigel Balchin: *The Small Back Room*
F.L. Green: *Odd Man Out*
(The last two were filmed.)

Apart from a few painful injections in my buttock, it was a relaxing month that I spent in Hampstead General. And the condition of my eye did improve to some extent (due more to the Guinness than to the injections, I am sure), although it never left me completely, and till today, more than sixty-five years later, my right eye clouds up whenever I'm a little run-down or under the weather. When I feel better, it clears up! It's rather like a barometer, indicating sunny days or gloomy days, responding to the state of my mind and body.

You learn to live with some things. And the human body can put up with a lot, provided you don't push it too far.

6

GONE WITH THE WIND

'Gone with the wind'—the line comes from a beautiful poem by Ernest Dowson, a poet of the 1890s, who died in London at the age of thirty-two. Most of his poems were dedicated to a young waitress in an Italian restaurant in Soho. He was madly in love with her, but she married another, leaving him desolate.

> *Her lips, her eyes, all day became to me*
> *The shadow of a shadow utterly.*
> *All day mine hunger for her heart became*
> *Oblivion, until the evening came,*
> *And left me sorrowful, inclined to weep,*
> *With all my memories that could not sleep.*[2]

Poor Ernest! I could identify with him.

---

[2] Dowson, Ernest, The Poems And Prose Of Ernest Dowson, The Bodley Head, 1905. P. 33

A spring and summer of love, an autumn and winter of longing and despair . . .

Vu-Phuong was her name. She said that it meant 'like the wind'—and, like the wind, she came and went.

Gentle Vu, I loved you so and you were kind and loved me too.

She came from Vietnam, and she wasn't a waitress, although her sister in Paris did run a small café.

How did I meet her? I really can't remember. Chance brought her into my life, and chance took her out of it. We make friends for life—even when distant, their presence is felt—but love, even true love, is unpredictable.

It must have been Thanh who introduced her to me. He was a Vietnamese student who wanted to improve his English. He cultivated my friendship in the mistaken belief that if he spent a lot of time with me, he would acquire a posh British accent. By the time he realised his error—

my accent being far from British or posh—it was too late, he had acquired an Indian accent!

Vu was quite happy with her Vietnamese-French accent and wasn't particularly interested in mine. She seemed to like my company, and when she discovered that I knew something about trees and plants and flowers, she sought me out, for she had a fascination for parks and formal gardens, and of course, London had a great many green spaces if you looked for them: Regent's Park, Primrose Hill, Hampstead Heath, Kensington Gardens, Kew Gardens! I'd been to most of them on some of my explorations of the city, and I was happy to take Vu around.

I still have a photograph of her. I did not have a camera; she gave it to me. Here she is, pretty and petite, well-turned-out, looking very composed. If I had to compare her to a flower, it would be a pale pink rose, a rose bud, just about to open—always on the verge of opening but never quite doing so.

On one of our walks, I plucked a daisy and placed it in her hair. Yes, she was made for flowers—a gentle wind in a field of nodding poppies.

We walked to the top of Primrose Hill and sat on the grass. I held her hand, and when we came downhill, we were still holding hands.

It did not take me long to fall in love with her.

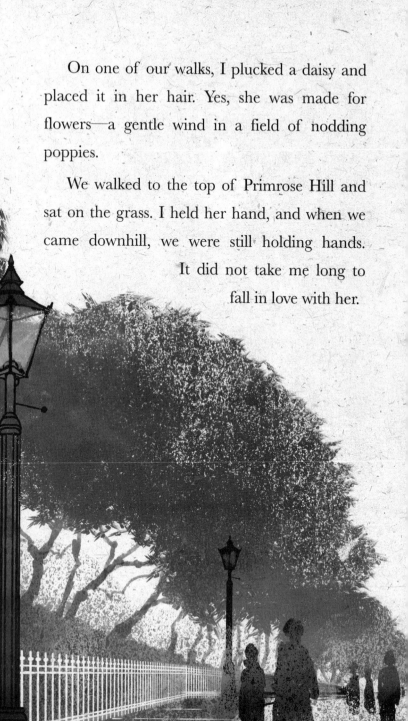

She took me to her room, cooked a meal for me and taught me how to use chopsticks. She taught me a couple of simple card games, and also how to tell someone's fortune from the tea leaves and the pattern they made at the bottom of a teacup when the tea had been finished. We used tea leaves there, not teabags.

Most of all, I looked forward to our excursions, for then I could tell her the names of unfamiliar plants and flowers, and experience a feeling of being wanted.

For what else could I offer her? Her people, back in Vietnam, were fairly affluent, although that affluence was in danger of being swamped by the approaching prospects of a communist Vietnam.

On a summer day, we went down to Kew Gardens, south of the river. Vu was charmed by the spacious lawns and bluebells growing along the sidewalls. I felt at home in the massive greenhouses, walking amongst tropical plants. The warmth and humidity made me long for the land I'd left behind.

'I feel homesick just standing here,' I said. 'It must have been like this in Vietnam.'

'I don't remember that home,' said Vu. 'I was very young when we left. I grew up in Paris. I don't know if I would ever see Vietnam.'

'Well, I will certainly go back to India,' I said. 'Home is the place of your heartiest memories—like these creepers, their fronds, these palms, these giant leopard lilies. Would you like to come with me?'

'You come with me to Paris!' she said, laughing. 'I'll teach you French.'

'First teach me how to cook,' I said.

And she did teach me how to cook, but I wasn't very good at it, always adding too many spices, due no doubt to my Indian upbringing.

I wanted to spend every weekend with her, and felt terribly lonely and lost if she could not always be with me. It was a long time since I had known the companionship of a girl of my age, and I was afraid of losing it. I made the mistake of being too intense, too relentless in my desire to be with her. She needed her own space.

When her college closed for the summer break, she announced that she was going strawberry-picking with a bunch of students. They would live on a farm for a fortnight, gather strawberries and be paid for their efforts.

'You don't need the money,' I said.

'No, but it will be fun!'

Fun for Vu and misery for me.

I grew extremely restless waiting for the strawberry month to pass.

Beware of falling in love, my friend. Everything else comes to a stop. Stories don't get finished. Friends are neglected. You are late for work and make mistakes with figures and balance sheets. You forget to have your beans on toast in the lunch break. You drink too much sherry in the evening. You stay awake all night.

Finally, you buy a ticket to Kintbury, a village in Berkshire, where Vu and her friends are spending their holidays working for a farm.

You get off the train at Kintbury. No one else gets off; it's a typical English village, the land where you meet Miss Marple in the only grocery shop. There is also an inn, an old-fashioned inn, straight out of *The Pickwick Papers*. Or better still, Surtees. On the walls are prints of horses and hounds, riders blowing bugles, and fleeing foxes. The hunt is on!

After a beer and a ham sandwich, I inquire the way to the strawberry farm. The landlord obliges, and I set off through the village—two villages, in fact—and a cluster of farm buildings, and a fallow field where I am chased by a bad-tempered bull.

I am surrounded by a gaggle of girls, some foreign, some very English—and there among them is Vu, happy as a lark, if indeed larks are happy.

'What brings you here?' she asked.

'You, of course! I was feeling bored, so I came to see you.'

'Well, here I am.'

'Enjoying yourself?'

'Having a wonderful time. But you can't join us; it's only for students.'

'No, that's all right,' I said. 'I just thought I'd drop by. Phone me when you're back in town. Bye, Vu.'

'Bye, Ruskin.'

And I trudged back to the inn, had another beer and sandwich, and caught the next train that stopped at Kintbury. I was feeling more miserable than ever, but at least I'd seen an English village.

*

The holidays and the strawberry season were over, but there was no word from Vu. I phoned the girls' hostel where she had been staying, and was told that she had gone to stay with friends in Tooting. That was in South London, far from my North London lodging. But I made inquiries from Thanh and all the students I knew, and I was able to get her address. And down to Tooting I went, like a lovesick, lovelorn Ernest Dowson—and not even a poem to woo her with!

I knocked on the door of the address I'd been given. It was opened by an unfriendly character who looked a bit like Peter Lorre, the insidious spy of many a Warner Brothers epic. Was Vu at home? I asked. No one by that name lived there, he told me, and shut the door. I walked across the road and stood on the opposite pavement, waiting— but waiting for what?

Was I becoming a stalker? It was obvious that Vu did not want to see me.

As it grew dark, the lights in the house came on. Up on the top floor, a figure was silhouetted against the window. It could have been Vu. In fact, I was sure it was her.

Had she tired of me so soon?

Was I too importunate a lover? Or had something else, some family pressure, forced her to stay

away? Whatever the reason, I felt unwanted, cheapened. I walked away, perhaps already knowing that my emotional life lay elsewhere.

It took me some time to resign myself to the disappointment, to this sudden end to a loving relationship. There was no one to confide in, that was the trouble. I could hardly unburden myself to my landlady—or to my publisher for that matter. And the students I knew were Vu's friends, not mine.

But I would not brood forever. I was now twenty, and life was full of possibilities.

7

LISTEN TO YOUR HEART

But it's a long, long while

From May to December.

And the days grow short

When you reach September.

'September Song' by Walter Huston, my favourite song . . . The plane trees were losing their leaves, the chrysanthemums in Kensington Gardens were beginning to droop and lose their vigour.

It was a time for reflection.

Diana took me to St Paul's to a recital given by Yehudi Menuhin, the great violinist. The last time I'd seen and heard a violin being played was in my prep school days in Shimla when our headmaster, the hated Mr Priestly, would practise on his violin every evening outside our dormitory

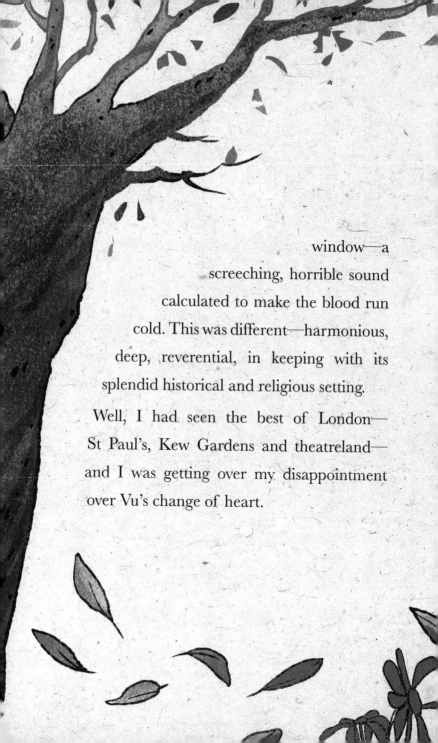

window—a
screeching, horrible sound
calculated to make the blood run
cold. This was different—harmonious,
deep, reverential, in keeping with its
splendid historical and religious setting.

Well, I had seen the best of London—
St Paul's, Kew Gardens and theatreland—
and I was getting over my disappointment
over Vu's change of heart.

Sorrowful, inclined to weep, I was now beginning to sleep again and dream of other things.

But André couldn't make up his mind about publishing my novel. He had shown it to another 'reader', Laurie Lee, the author of *Cider with Rosie*, who had said that publishing it would be a gamble, but that he wouldn't blame them for taking it. Publishers did gamble in those days if a writer showed talent. At the same time, they did not relish losing money on a book, and I was the first to admit that *The Room on the Roof*,

so personal a story, was unlikely to be a runaway bestseller. All the same, I could not wait forever! I wrote to André and Diane, saying it was time they made up their minds, and that if they couldn't, they should return my manuscript without delay.

Over the years, I have had tiffs with my publishers, and this was the first of them.

André sent me a contract and a cheque for £50, which was the standard advance in those days. But it would be about a year before the book

came out, I was told. Another long wait for the impatient young author. But now I could boast of being an author, instead of just a writer; an author being someone who'd written a book, though yet to be published! Young authors who are in a hurry to get published should not look upon me as someone who had an immediate success. I was seventeen when I started my novel and twenty-one by the time I received my first copy (when I was back in India)!

*

I had been restless for some time, angry with myself for botching up my relationship with Vu. I could only blame myself for being so clumsy, so impatient.

Also, London was a lonely city, and I had no close friend. If you wanted to meet people, you had to join a club, and I wasn't the clubby type. I travelled to the Photax office every day, and in the evening, I would come back to my tiny room and write a little. On weekends, I would go to a cinema or theatre, and almost always ended up eating at cheap restaurants. 'Meat and two veg'—that was the standard fare. Or you could vary it with beans on toast.

My job in Photax was a dull, dreary affair. My fellow clerks were always decent to me, but when the office closed, they were all eager to get away, catch their trains to distant suburbs, hurry homewards and then rush back to town the following morning. I think I was the only one who lived within a reasonable distance. Half an hour in the tube, and I was in Hampstead. But no one was waiting for me at home, so I would go out again for a frugal supper.

I had grown up in a small town in north India, where you knew almost everyone who lived in your vicinity. Some became friends; others went about their business, but there were no strangers. Perhaps it was time to return to the familiar lanes and bazaars and mango groves of Dehradun, or the pine-clad slopes of Shimla and Mussoorie.

Had I stayed on in England, would I have become a more successful writer? I have often been asked that question. But I think I did the right thing! I followed my heart instead of my head. It is something I have done all my life. It may not have made for wealth, but it has certainly made for happiness.

And besides, everything that I wrote and would write stemmed from my Indian life. I felt immersed in India, something I had never felt in England.

Out of my £50 advance, £40 bought me a ticket back to India, a three-week voyage in the good ship MS *Batory*, a Polish steamer that sailed between Europe and the East on a fairly regular basis.

I did not tell anyone I was leaving. Diana would hear from me when I was back in Dehradun. I had, of course, to give a week's notice to my employer, and they said they were sorry to see me go. But I would be replaced within a week; just another clerk who vanished into the wilderness of thousands of city offices.

Two suitcases held all my belongings. One of them is still with me, a cheap cardboard suitcase I'd bought in Jersey. It is about to fall apart (after

over sixty-five years of service), but I use it to store away old manuscripts and scrapbooks.

Struggling with my suitcases, I boarded the good ship *Batory*, only to find that its departure had been delayed because some of the crew had sought political asylum in Britain. It was that kind of ship, and it seemed unwilling to make the voyage.

The crew replenished, we got under way, only to be stuck in Gibraltar for a couple of days because of further desertions.

Then, at Port Said, after a day of sightseeing, two passengers failed to return to the ship. We sailed without them.

It was a long voyage, and I wrote two stories, one about an old steamer that used to visit the small port of Jamnagar when I was a small boy. It was called 'Faraway Places'. I forget the other. But I wasn't wasting time. There was no job waiting for me in India, and I knew I would have to make a living with my pen.

In the Red Sea, in the middle of the night, someone jumped overboard. The ship stopped and a boat was lowered, but he wasn't found. A wag said it was the ship's captain; the crew was very secretive about it.

It was March 1955, and it was growing hotter by the day. I loved the heat, I soaked it up. 'For the rain it raineth every day,' sang Shakespeare, in praise of the English climate. And he was welcome to it, with a hey-nonny-no!

I stood at the ship's railing, watching the palm-framed shores of India as they heaved into sight, and I knew I wouldn't be leaving them again.

ACKNOWLEDGEMENTS

The author wishes to thank Sohini Mitra, Simran Kaur, Aditi Batra and Samar Bansal for helping shape this memoir, and Mihir Joglekar for his lively and evocative illustrations.

Read More in the Series

Looking for the Rainbow: My Years with Daddy

At age eight, Ruskin escapes his jail-like boarding school in the hills and goes to live with his father in Delhi. His time in the capital is filled with books, visits to the cinema, music and walks and conversations with his father— a dream life for a curious and wildly imaginative boy, which turns tragic all too soon.

For years, Ruskin Bond has regaled and mesmerized readers with his tales. In *Looking for the Rainbow*, Bond travels to his own past, recalling his favourite adventures (and misadventures) with extraordinary charm, splotches of wit, a pinch of poignance and not a trace of bitterness.

What you're holding, dear reader, is a classic in the making.

Read More in the Series

Till the Clouds Roll By: Beginning Again

A couple of years after his father's death, ten-year-old Ruskin travels to Dehradun to spend his holidays with his new family. As he reacquaints himself with his mother, now remarried and with a busy social life, his stepfather and new siblings, a pensive Ruskin longs for his father's company, his stamp collection and the old gramophone. Trying to escape this unfamiliar place, he immerses himself in books and explores the forest glades, canals and bazaars of the little town, forming some unlikely friendships on the way.

After the much-loved *Looking for the Rainbow*, the master storyteller lends another backward glance at his boyhood years—a vacation that took place over seventy winters ago—remembering his days with rare humour, remarkable charm and twinges of heartache.